PRACTICAL ANXIETY

The publisher gratefully acknowledges the support of the Canada Council for the Arts and the Ontario Arts Council for its publishing program. The publisher is also grateful for the financial assistance received from the Government of Canada.

Front cover artwork: Jian Jun An, "The thirsty crow," 2009, acrylic on canvas, 29" x 30", artist website: www.jianjunan.com.

Library and Archives Canada Cataloguing in Publication

Greco, Heidi, author
          Practical anxiety / Heidi Greco.

(Inanna poetry & fiction series)
Poems.
ISBN 978-1-77133-581-2 (softcover)

          I. Title. II. Series: Inanna poetry and fiction series

PS8563.R41452P73 2018   C811'.6   C2018-904381-4

Printed and bound in Canada

Inanna Publications and Education Inc.
210 Founders College, York University
4700 Keele Street, Toronto, Ontario M3J 1P3 Canada
Telephone: (416) 736–5356   Fax (416) 736–5765
Email: inanna.publications@inanna.ca Website: www.inanna.ca

PRACTICAL ANXIETY

For Isabella,
With thanks for
letting me be part of
Muriel's Journey — and
yours!

POEMS BY

HEIDI GRECO

Inanna Poetry & Fiction Series

INANNA Publications and Education Inc.
Toronto, Canada

For Jane, who understood

Contents

GOOGLING FOR JESUS

EARTH AS IT IS

INTO THE LIGHT

MOUNTAINS TO CROSS

In the high heavens,
The ageless places,
The gods are wringing their great worn hands
For their watchman is away, their world-engine
Creaking and cracking.
—W. H. Auden, *The Age of Anxiety*

A String of Worry Beads

Oh dear angel

The picture in the book: Dick and Jane beside their house.
Jane in a polka-dot dress, balanced
on clip-on skates, wobbling pigeon-toed
rolling toward the road.

She's grabbed the criss-crossed straps
of Dick's blue coveralls. His feet turn
endless circles with the pedals of his trike,
inscribing on the driveway eternal figure eights.

Jane's rosy cheeks reveal a healthy disposition,
but the dog behind her leaps, yips a warning.
The words he tries to shape rise in cartoon-round balloons
filled with exclamation marks, excited good-dog barks.

Meanwhile, here comes Father, dutifully leaving for work,
wearing his wide-brimmed brown fedora.
Looking straight ahead with steely Father-eyes,
he backs the black sedan from the garage.

A pink-gowned guardian angel hovers
just behind the children. Looking bored,
she stands on air, the hem of her dress a whirring blur,
holds in her fingers a thick cigar, the tip of it hottest orange.

Land of the Sugar Plum Fairies

Quilt to my chin in the darkened room, told it was time for sleep,
I would try to stay awake. But soon the plucking violins
would fill my ears, surround me: frightening tiptoe music of their
   dance.

Every time I closed my eyes they'd be floating
near the ceiling: Sugar-dusted faces, purpled
skin like a deepening bruise. Rounded howling mouths
that whistled with the wind, singing to the snow outside,
white and piling higher, glowing with a cold blue light,

waiting in their tutus to leap onto the covers, grab me,
take me to their snowplace far away.

> A castle cold and hidden
> behind walls of crystal ice.
> Only one could help me home
> a snowman prisoner there,
> the grin of his empty mouth gone slack
> and I had to bring him to life.

> A hard wrinkled walnut served as his heart
> the trick was to dig out a hole with my fingers,
> shove its dark wood
> into the chill of his body.

It all comes back as a fever sometimes will.
An overheated Christmas day
the kitchen one big oven smell
dinner at my grandma's, all of us
cousins running around. And still I can't remember
whether I was in some movie,
or if it really happened when I gouged the walnut, beating,
pulled it for him, from my open chest.

Doc Robin

How serious the robins look jumping across the lawn
feet together tight, like practice for a sack race.

But when they stop and listen, tilt their heads in search of worms
it's then I think of stethoscopes, tiny, 'round their necks.

Was there some old book somewhere, picture of a summer bird
looking wise and doctorly, in one of those headband things?

Its concave silver mirror surely would have shown
the terror in my gaze as he checked his long syringe

the single drop of water bleeding from its tip and then
its needle, sharpened beak, biting the bone of my arm

while in my mind I cocked my head,
listened, hopped with pain.

Being seven: one who names

These are her lunch hours, second row pew,
kneeling, barely visible in the candle-lit church.
Away from the playground's push-and-shove noise,
heaving dodgeballs, scowling boys. Here
no twirling girls with skipping-ropes can taunt her.

Only stained glass watches her, casting prismed light,
with scattered flocks of cherubs, small apostles, rosy-cheeked
babies with dimpled knees and lightly feathered wings.

She understands their faces, has given
all of them names – *Angela, Sunshine, Pinky.*
She's met one sure to be her baby brother.

Stillbirth, they said, though she doesn't like that word.
Much too quiet, much too soft for what she hears at night –
crying and shouting and swearing bad words –
and somehow forgetting to give him a name.

She likes to call him *Christopher,* like the statue she has seen.
He carries baby Jesus high above the waters,
safe up on his shoulder from the river and its floods.

Christopher. A name she thinks a baby would like,
a name that makes the easing sound of whispers.
The name she says inside her head
while she rounds the circular loops,
trying to focus holy thoughts on her rosary beads,
Hail Mary, Hail Mary, Hail Mary.

She knows how long it takes to unravel the string of words:
Mary times ten, Our Father between, the whole series over
times five. Then back to the start, spin it again
like a fairy's magic spell, times three.

A formula that eats exactly thirty-seven minutes,
leaving ninety seconds to be outside for the bell, then sneak
(a ghost, like her brother) to the back of the double-file line.
Ready to go inside for lessons, camouflaged almost enough,
just another uniformed girl, one of the squirming Grade Threes.

Geneses

A carpet of black sagged the roof
of the abandoned warehouse,
the one down by the edge of the lake
blocking the line of the view.

When the blackness surged,
a single body moving,
my uncle wagged his eyebrows,
breathed a secret, told me
that it was a convention
for all the flies on earth, making
important plans before they flew away
spreading germs everywhere in the world.

Then took another puff of his smelly brown cigar,
squinted at me through a fog of smoke, nodding

and I believed.

Don't tell

Do you remember that fridge,
standing in the open field
the one that gave us terrible dreams
through August and July?

How, finally, we got up the nerve
daring each other,
who would go first,
pry at its rusted door.

The idea of a body,
cold and stiff and blue
falling out and into the deep green grass.

Those quiet speculations we had about a boy
picturing how he'd fit himself, crouching
hide-and-seek, into squared-off corners
pale and silent.

The worst part, imagining
after he was hidden, counting in the dark
up to a hundred,

then more sets of one hundreds, rounds
of number prayers,

with no one coming, nobody
looking anymore. All gone home for

suppertime, no one able to hear
his bloody fists thumping the metal door.

And later when he understood
his secret was forever amen.

Chasing the Light of Fireflies

for Helen Humphreys

There's a photo of me, curled now at the edges, black & white and grainy, but clear enough to tell that I am chasing fireflies. Chubby fingers reaching as I stumble after them, who could know whether I managed to touch one.

By school years we caught them in the bowl of our bedtime hands, positioned them into wide-mouthed jars, ones our mother saved for us, Miracle Whip. Our dad would pound a nail, make holes in the lid for air. We'd add beds of grass and clover, food to last the night. Always, by morning, they'd be still as darkened stones.

As teens out to impress, we tore the glowing bugs apart, scraped mean smears of yellow-green onto the thighs of our pants, sometimes added X's cross our cheeks. Imagining things we might do to each other, fires of our summery young love.

Pencils and pointers

I always held my pencil wrong
tangled in my fingers
angled close against the page
too low for the teacher to see.

I knew answers to questions
I wasn't supposed to know
yet couldn't speak when it came my turn
to say them.

Too often I'd have escaped
in clouds outside the window,
lost to pictures in library books:
exploding ships with reddened sails,
the Spanish Armada up in flame, splinters
flying into the thick
fingers of pointing tornadoes.

And sometimes I'd get caught up
scribbling on my desk
secret words and messages
between the zigzag lines
someone else had gouged into
the unforgiving wood.

Cheese Leg

A hot August day when I met the girl with the wooden leg. Covered in pinkish paint, it wore a real sock and its own black shoe, cute with a shiny thin strap that closed with a button.

I remember the way she walked, as if rowing a boat on land, rolling as she navigated the cracks of the buckled sidewalk. Still, her smile looked nice, and I was glad when she approached where I sprawled beneath the shadow of a tree. Her sitting down looked complicated, a kind of stiff unfolding, but leaning into the tree, she inched along the grass toward me.

Our mothers were in the butcher shop, the store where I hated the smell. Every time we went there, I begged to wait outside. The girl said she didn't like the smell either, but giggled, asked what I was scared of, teasing that a smell could never hurt you.

I said I hated those loud laughing men, so fat in their red-smeared aprons, bits of meat on the blades of their shining knives. How their butchering eyes looked mean, as if they might like to take a chunk of me, hang it in their dark back room, the one with the big locking handle.

Both of us were quiet then, the only sound the buzz of a bee or a fly, and all I could do was stare at the chips of pink paint flaking off her leg, peeling as if they were melting in the heat of that summer day. But before I could ask anything, my mother marched out, ordered me to hurry and get in the car.

Still at night I worry that something tunnels inside my leg – fat tore-do worms, carving Swiss-cheese shapes in muscle and bone. And I think about that girl – like me, now grown to woman – and wonder if I scared her more than her leg frightened me.

Chinook

one of those impossible January days
warm enough to be April, even May

on the playground, kids are tossing
their jackets in a pile, a few

still wear them tied
around their waist, but

nobody is wasting this
unexpected heat, except perhaps

the brown-haired girl, sitting
in the toilet stall, looking

at the red mistake
smeared on her underpants

only this morning
they were so white.

The Mathematics of Anxiety

The Uncertainty of Machines

It's funny, don't you think, how time seems to do a lot of things? It flies, it
tells, and worst of all, it runs out.—Markus Zusak

The shining ivory weighscale, deco lines all smoothly curved
tall as Tut's sarcophagus, tucked into the corner
its creaminess so out of sync with the glare of the bright arcade
noise and screaming light effects: hyper-active neon.

You could read the bold inscription on the front of the machine
engraved in curling letters on the narrow brass plate:
one cent honest measure, a solemn-sounding vow.

I drop the copper into the slot and wait
for a response: deliberations, moving gears
grind from deep within. Heavy and slow,
they settle their teeth, mesh into place with a moan.

Calibrated finite lines etched in equal degree
show my weight in kilograms, pounds and even stone.
I select the clever sound of ten stone, eleven
preferring it to the thud of a hundred and fifty-one.

I fret at sinister dangers: chance of faucets being reversed,
installed by left-handed plumbers in a hurry. Am anxious
I might scald myself while fiddling half in sleep, fumbling
in the sink at night, to fill my hand with water.

Hazardous

Cleaning old grass from inside the mower blades
pulling at the dried bits, gone hard as *papier maché*
they hold a rounded helmet shape, the shell
of the machine, as if remembering something
I should not forget.

And all the while I focus my
attention on the blade, quiet
with the cord unplugged, yet

I can feel the heart of the engine, chattering, still warm
as if it might be ready
            to leap back into life
take a slice of my finger
keep it as its own.

A murder of crows, a flicker of hummingbirds

This morning, overanxious over trying
to quit smoking, I remember stinging words
that flew from our mouths last night, squawking
like a murder of crows, or murderous anyway.
We'd hurled them, sharp as knives
aglint in the gathering storm, grumbling
like crumbling thunderheads, prolonging
our long fall out of love.

I obsess over polishing, overpolishing a window
the one overlooking the messy patch of scrub
but leave the others dirty, streaked with old rain, befitting
the kind of grudge I am working on today.

Thump! a hummingbird dives into the glass
drives his beak far as the back of his brain.

I bend to pick him from the grass, struggling
blades of northern lee, hold him in my hand
a perfect comma, pausing the day.

He fits the bowl of my palm, still
shimmers green to gold, iridescent
rainbows crowning his skull.
A shudder of breath rearranges the colours
that cross his miniature breast, then
one precise jewel appears, red from his open mouth
and the fluttering ceases, empty.

Only my size marks me different from him
that and the fact my two-kilo brain
lies heavier in my head than before.

I have held death in my open hand,
the lightest birdweight lingers
somewhere near my wrist,
an added pulse courses through my blood.

The tip of a beak has left its mark
a new line added to swirls on my palm:
one more truth to bear in memory,
one more scar to wear into tomorrow.

Stranger, at Banff

Mountains here, too near my window
make me feel enclosed.

Even the breath in my lungs seems to catch
dry as dusty moths, fluttery
and lost in the cave of my chest.

This claustrophobic landscape
cradles us carelessly, as if it were the palm
of some apathetic god.

I half-expect the hand to close
curl upon itself, unforgiving
fist of stone, eternal.

Practical Anxiety

A groaning from the floorboards might mean today's the day
to pound some nails, glue some joists, not just worry nighttimes,
wondering what's been eating them hollow from below: insects
or a spreading damp at work in moulding beams.

The brothers passed the weekend playing games of rummy
sliding cards back and forth beneath the bedroom door,
closed, so the one boy wouldn't catch his brother's measles,
another of those could-be-deadly childhood diseases.

Our overflowing pantry holds too many rows of soups,
more than we might consume over the coldest winters.
Scattered about are batteries, bottles filled with water,
flashlights standing on end, promises cold as empty vases.

Pinkest strains of maybe-blood in yesterday morning's pee,
a twitching under the eye that's probably something worse,
a hardening that tomorrow might become a dangerous lump,
somewhere lurking nasty, out of sight.

Admiration, divisible by

I've always admired twelve – the number, itself.
Such elegance: one-one plus one equalling one-two.
The one-two punch, that one-two start to any counting up.

All those easy factors, nearly everyone in tow: one, two, three, four,
six, and twelve. Back to twelve again. Even by another name: dozen,
two-plus-ten, *duodecim,* it's still twelve. Two times fresh eggs in a row,

beers for Friday night. Doughnuts, maybe hot dog buns,
bagels, brownies, oatmeal squares, plates
lined down the table for Thanksgiving.

Twelve the golden number,
children running
in the yard.

In Defense of Messiness

There is something to be said for the open sweep of an unmade bed,
rumpled from the tumble of early morning love. For the skeltered
pile of unwashed glasses, food-stained forks and plates, souvenirs
of last night's drawn-out laughter.

Pieces of a puzzle strewn across the wooden table – their mix of
sprawling colours unlikely as the sea. Haphazardness of outline,
each shape curling on itself, looking for its mate amongst the blues,
all those improbable bites of sky. How much more compelling these
random broken bits than the finished square, mirroring the boredom
of the image on the box.

So much to be said for the chaos of things, how better this state of
endless ongoing entropy. Left to its boisterous ways, everything gets
messier, stickier – only more delicious. O for the happy slurry of life
than a house gone too quiet, too clean.

Women understand the colour red

We see it every month, breathe
its metal scent,
a part of us rolling out, to answer the call of moon.

No wonder we redden our lips
blush at the mention of kisses
covet russet highlights in our hair

wear scarlet bandannas, red silken skirts
swirl in a blurring dance of madder
wiggle our hips, *olé!*

Spring Camp, Deep Creek

Setting up the tent was a lesson in disaster
watching the pegs roll down the hill, lost

down the mouth of the green ravine, all we could do was watch
as they toppled their way to the sea.

Wind bit into our backs as we wrestled
the bundle of shining cloth, entangling

ourselves in a complicated web: bungees
and fabric and string.

Flap-flapping, the thin skin sang through the night,
how the leathered wings of pterodactyls might sound

soaring above us, outstretched while we slept,
safe in the silence of love.

Poem of X, Y, and Z

for Robert G

X marks the spot where I sit on the bus
you are sitting Y in the seat behind
I am reading a book called something like Z
when you interrupt with a quiet remark
how stunningly lovely the day.

Next thing I know, you
are showing me photos
black & whites from long ago, the '80s.
You tell me it's your stepson who's squinting from behind
a sandpile at some park – quite the creation:
Mt St Helen's at his feet, complete with caved-in sides.

You explain your ADHD
tell me your theories on it
a manifestation of PTSD,
say that your mind's inflamed.
You say your eyes are too full of horror
bad things that happen to people you love,
every laneway waiting in betrayal.

I suggest you try EMDR
better than LSD, much smoother
than MDA, our fragmented DNA
these letters we toss around
because they are lighter than words.

Bus ride Sunday morning
the world of our knowing each other
sufficient to make me think in terms
of X and Y and Z. Such fragile convergences,
enough to make me write these words
to see if I can thank you
for helping me see.

Gravity of the Situation:
Stuck in the Elevator of the Lee Building

(Vancouver, Main at Broadway)

nothing we can do but wait
inside this dangling box, stuck
between these floors that mutter
stories that no longer matter

the rotating billboard high on the roof
keeps showing its jaded face
selling lottery promos
to another Friday night
worn as any hooker
standing outside by the bus
hoping to meet a trick who will break
the steadiness of rain
            (all of us wish we'd thought to bring wine
            bags of salt snacks to help pass the time)

hanging by these dusty cables
closer to heaven than any of us wish,
holding on by breath of angels or worse,
I picture the rooftop billboard turning

some key for an antique wind-up toy
imagine it cranking us slowly down
a cradle as soft as crumbled clay
that line this building's walls. I wait
for the wakening rumble, beating heart of the ancient beast:
the tired machine that will grind its gears, manouevre

old pulleys, shift leaden weights. I think of how it will groan
as it places us where we belong, the way we will step out gingerly
the light-slicked surface of rain-rinsed streets
how we will walk away as if nothing has happened.

Googling for Jesus

Heaven is someplace and no place we know

So where exactly is heaven, he insists, blowing into the bowl of her ear, pushing too close from behind where she stands at the sink. *You're the Poet.*

She shakes him off, but still hears the laugh that followed him out the door, feels its greasy smarm worm its way into her spine. Still, she continues the task of clearing the evening's debris, channels the fuel of her heat to the water, swirls the cloth in soapy rounds, careening figure eights – these thin-stemmed crystal glasses have heard it all before.

Scrubbing each white dinner plate, she stands them aslant in the rack, a chorus with their silent golden rings.

She takes solace from cutlery, admires the resilience of metal, finds herself enjoying the dimpled indention of spoons, considers the relative uses of knives, wielders of final pronouncements.

Turning to where her questioner stood, she dries her hands and speaks to the room: *Heaven exists in a bubble of soap. Its waters are greyish and warm. Like clouds expectant with rain in July, sweet as a lazy day's nap.*

Switching off the kitchen light, she remembers the way she used to push the skin by the side of her eye, how the act seemed to magnify, sharpen her range of vision – blurred faces from the moon, dust motes in sunlight in late afternoon – all those bits of heaven, right between the eyes.

Stigmata

The other day there was this guy
sitting at my bus stop, but I could tell
he wasn't really waiting for a bus.

He asked if he could bum a smoke,
did I have one I could spare, yet
didn't seem to mind when I told him I had quit.

Still, I fished inside my purse, found
some heavy coins, held them in my open hand,
a guilty selfish gift.

He took them, thanked me in exchange
offered this advice: *Jesus was a spaceman
and he's coming for us soon.*

*He'll be looking for his kindred,
those who love him, those who follow.
He'll take us in his ship into the sky.*

Then asked if I could help him choose
which hand to show Jesus, which one
more convincing, the mark of true belief.

He opened both his fists, unfurling
burns from cigarettes, writ against his palms
a secret code: still-bleeding holes.

Then squinted at me, spoke again, wanting
me to know: *Jesus was a spaceman
and he's coming for us soon.*

In the name of the Lord: three scenes

Galilee, 33 AD:
Jesus, wearing a sign proclaiming him Lord,
rides astride an ass through a crowd. People
throw palms onto the road beneath him.

Europe, 1432:
An ass, proclaiming himself Lord,
rides astride a throne being carried through crowded streets. People
throw themselves beneath him, raise their palms, beg a sign of mercy.

North America, 2016:
Raising his palms to the spotlight, he proclaims himself
a gift to the people from Lord Jesus. The crowd, an unthinking ass,
throw signs up bearing his name.

When God Came to Stay with Us

We were camping, just my mum and me, when I first saw him.
There, plain as daylight was his face – looking through the screen fly
of the tent. Even though I'd heard he was watching all the time, being
smack in his eye like that made me know it had to be true.

The birds were singing like crazy, but my mother was still asleep,
making this grumbly snorting noise (she couldn't help it, mossy
smells got to her). I was being quiet as I could, touching myself a
bit. I guess God must have seen the covers jiggling from my hand
underneath, 'cause he crinkled his face in a smile and winked at me.

Funny, he didn't look at all like in the God-books at church. He had
blondish hair, cut pretty short and he looked kind of round-eyed
amazed, the way my uncle sometimes looks after a couple of beers.
Truthfully, he looked like a bit of a goof. But a nice one.

After that, I got kind of used to having him around. Like they say,
he's always there, watching. It doesn't have to change anything. It's
just the way he is. Somebody you want to leave a space for around
your campfire. Somebody that makes you want to look and maybe
wink back.

Trilogy for Faith, Hope and Charity

i. A Statement of Faith

Even at three this afternoon, a curtain of fog endures, blocking
my view of shoreline across the bay. Still, I expect

the land remains, although it's out of sight. Like Columbus
envisioning faraway worlds, I count on its existence

trust it will be there, along the horizon
when I look across the water, some other tomorrow.

ii. Hope is

an orange balloon
tied onto a skinny wrist

lifting
ever so slightly

lifting

iii. A Parable on Charity

When the ship descended onto the beach, everyone suspected a
publicity stunt. High-flying machines emitting loud whirring noises
often meant free samples of something new and addictive. Bags of
green potato chips chemically-induced. Coloured bottles of water to
clutter the landfill. Remarkable plastic plates overflowing with
canapés, covered with mounds of olives chopped into red-eyed rings.

Whatever was going to be passed out, everyone wanted their share.
So the teeming crowd pushed forward, bodies rolling over sand,
steady as an incoming tide pursuing the trilling sound.

When a man who looked like Jesus stepped through a sliding door,
the people looked disappointed, for they saw he bore nothing in his
hands – save for small red holes which he held high for all to see.

On seeing the discontent shimmering in every face, he spoke in
a voice that carried his words far and over the water, calming the
crowd and even the thrashing surf as it rode its horses to shore:
*If it will make them happy, let them eat chocolate, for nothing else matters
any more.*

Beatitudes for the 21st Century

(based on the Gospel of Matthew, 5: 3-10)

Blessed are the downtrodden,
for they shall be looked up to.

Blessed are the atheists,
for they shall be proven correct.

Blessed are the recyclers,
for their spirits shall dwell in trees.

Blessed are those who challenge the courts and question the greedy,
for they shall be affirmed.

Blessed are the orangutans, whose intelligence shall be acknowledged;
the horses, who shall rise in the sky, flying as they were intended;
the tortoises, who will be assigned more spacious dwellings.

Blessed are the sweet-natured,
for they shall come back as bees.

Blessed are the homeless, the addicted, the unemployed,
for they shall be granted overtime and ensconced amongst stars.

Blessed are those worn down by the blights of daily life,
for they shall be released to ride galaxies of light.

Earth As It Is

Green Tara intones the first notes of dawn in the forest

(remembering Sam Hamill)

ten fingers
ten toes
balance
five and five

Basho sings praise
his body has nine holes
to capture morning birdsong

I harmonize
the song of ten holes

Portrait of a Forest

Begin
with a single tree
alone in a grassy field.

Observe
the obstinate way its trunk
wrenches ever upward, sustained
by the very earth it pulls itself from.

Notice
the shape of its myriad branches
spreading out and open
like a waiting hand to cup the rain.

Consider
the line of its stance
how it reaches for the light
the ways it bends around itself, stretching into breeze.

Contemplate
the many years the tree has resided here
the many dried-up summers it has endured
the winter nights it's stood its ground
against the cold, in solitude.

Listen
to its branches, their tips so fine in green,

those many sibilant fingers, rubbing amongst themselves
a mystery of whisperings to the sky.

*

As a single tree can be admired,
a forest is to respect. So much more
than the sum of its trees, it lives
and breathes, holds the soil in its grasp
enmeshed in a handshake of intertwined roots.

It is essential, the same way
we must hold one another,
lean toward the lee, away from the wind.

Linked in

the long tall truths of trees
make such long strong boards
long gone, broad song I sing

I shudder at the sound of heavy machinery,
feel the grinding tune of chainsaws in my belly

brace myself for the thud of heavy branches falling,
blunted amputations, alive and growing.

If a tree falls in the forest, I know before I hear it.
Connected, I bleed for it inside.

Vanities of our Times

...The age of greed and waste.

—Marge Piercy

rusting trucks in a slow line
interspersed with tired buses
gear down with drawn-out farting sounds
snake their way from the jungle,
along the winding road, carrying
logs so newborn fresh, I imagine them streaked in blood

although their diameters reach wider
than my arms outstretched,
I know these trees will probably be mashed to pulp for paper –
throw-away diapers, toilet tissue, folding dollar bills,
or nothing more substantial
than flimsy words like these, light enough
to float on wind, disappear in a whim of flame.

Seasonal

This is the summer everyone but me
has fallen in love with the sun.

I have developed a tic in my eye
scanning the skies for even a wisp
        of cloud, possible rain

coolness to bless us, kiss
the parched mouth of earth.

Morning Commute, Vancouver

She swims along the freeway
beside the rest of the working-class fish, climbing
corporate ladders, half past six.

She paddles her outrigger hard against the tide
avoids getting caught in the counter-flow lane
gulps a breath and, lips compressed, holds it

       then barrels through the tunnel beneath the river's surge.

Emerging into sunlight, she's filled with sudden cravings,
a pull from low in her groin announces wild desires
more urgent than monthly paycheques, greater than nagging debris:
all those empty coffee cups strewn across the dash,
fast-food wrappers lining the floor, indulgences best forgotten.

Night of the Bears

While we slept our way across another wintry night,
you, my love, were saving bears
dreaming rescue schemes.

Devising aluminum islands for an ocean with no ice:
floating metal platforms for the polar bears to walk on
artificial stepping stones so they won't drown.

I see water dense with bears, nose to tip to nose,
like pieces in some Escher tessellation
swarming in a sea gone soupy warm.

Their whitish fur, slicked back smooth
makes them look like fish, thick
as schools of salmon used to be

spawning in some woodland stream,
dense enough for us to walk
carefully, on tiptoe cross their backs.

Perseids/Nebulae

After a night of too much sleep
but not enough rest, I stay,
dawdling in this bed so warm, loath to launch the day.

Instead I replay the muddle of dream
the two of us riding a sea canoe
paddling through a clutter of scum, gliding
a line that zags amidst a chocolate bar wrapper,
a cigarette pack, the sole
of a floating shoe.

Encountering a clear patch, we peer
into the shallows, strain to observe constellations
dwindling life below: swirls of purple starfish
adorned with too many arms, crabs who run insane
as if their heads have been chopped off,
churning spirals of ever-tightening circles.

Relentless

The day the tide rose, it swallowed the beach slowly
then crept along the bricks of the city promenade
fingered its way across the road, insinuating salty paths
between flower beds, lawn trolls, banks of tended roses.

It seeped into the depths of sturdy old foundations,
weeping thin trails down grey concrete walls
puddled the floors of garages, rearranging tools
signed its name with debris from overturned bins,
giving notice in a wake of scummy foam.

The Dreams We Take for Silence

Trees that leaned tall and sweet yesterday afternoon
are gone. All that new sky bleeding blue mocks me with its beauty.
Last week lilacs twelve feet tall were swirling their blossoms free in
   the wind,
scratching their names on the day, the cloud of their scent erasing
   any neighbours.

I remember when this was the field where Jevon and Peter played,
built their secret rocket ships, dreamt of who-knows-what
now it's overgrown with rows of identical homes
filled with anything-but-identical families.

The shortcuts and byways have all been replaced
by squared-off yards smoothed flat with lawns, trimmed
in conventional styles – just so many haircuts in a row –
no room left for envy when everything looks the same.

Everyone lies awake at night, aligned in their king-size beds,
clutching remotes instead of each other, tuned to the flickering
light with its pitches, while all they can do is dream,
tired but wide-eyed, thinking up one more gadget to buy.

River of salmon, river of dreams

glint of silver in the water
rides a freshet to the sea

1.
She's laid her cache of eggs in the secrecy of gravel
these private stones selected for the shadows falling here,
moving water, cool and sheltered, lively.

2.

An army of silvery fry ride currents, hurtle towards the sea
marking a route they will follow years from now.

Memorizing moss and ferns beside the water's edge,
fans of lacy cedar, boney hands of wild salal

reaching toward the frothing rush of stream.
A green rock looms, resembling the shadow of a bear.

Surface of river all a-whirl, a swirling of stars overhead,
moon's pale light a beacon to be learned.

3.
Estuary, a place to rest where river meets the sea
and ocean rises, rinsing itself, merging wet worlds.

This is where the smolts acquire their final polished glow,
where baptizing brine confers a name
with zing of salty tang: *saltfish, saltman, salmon.*

4.
Clans converge in the open sea: Adams, Cowichan, Elwha
each with ancestral tales, stories old as trees that rise
high as guiding stars, sprawling constellations to point the way.

Those from the Elwha a-chatter this year
dams and obstructions being un-built, finally
allowed to go home. The many years they've gathered
at the base of the concrete wall, remembering
promises made. They flick their tails,
swish off, dive deep, energy renewed.

5.
Rising scent of river mouth
the salmon run assembles

a horde of silvery murmurings
as chittering lips adjust

locate the almost-forgotten taste:
salt-less. Clarity of memory

stars and moonlight
dappled shadows, home.

6.
I dream of broken fish ladders
leading nowhere but sky.

Standing at a blackboard, a stream of long division,
a trail
      of numbers
          falling
               too many remainders.

Diagramming sentences, chalky fingers, breathing dust
Subject+Predicate\Complement
Habitat+Becomes\Endangered

Those are just the easy ones
that linger when I wake,
bathed in sweat as if I've been
thrusting my body upward,
hurling myself, stretching,
to climb the watery structure,

         falling back again,
   again,
again.

7.

As petals of rosiest tulips will fade,
turn pale as curls of withered skin, droop,

the homing salmon's hue will rise,
sides as bright as if aflame, blood-ruddy,

will ride the beat of pounding waters
battle fearsome currents, calming

only when the milt is spread,
the future laid down.

8.
habit
in.habit
habit/ation
habitant

inhabitant:
their habit to return
to old habits at
their habitat

habit
uninhabit
uninhabitable
un.habitat

9.
fungus-spotted corpses

    float

        down

            stream

            whirling

        eddies

10.
One two three four five
Once I saw a fish alive.
Six seven eight nine ten
Will I see one yet again?

Walking inventory, end of November

one torn-down sign: *free bed/only*
      used 1 yr.
four takeaway coffee cups: Tim Horton's,
Seattle's Best, Starbucks, Mocha Café

eighty cigarette butts before I lose
count, enough to light up too many lungs
with cancer

zero empty bottles, the gleaners
have been through, each
trolling private territories
through the darkened streets, clinking
oh-so quietly, well before the dawn

five leggy dandelions, golden
of throat, lean back, ready to play
some final trumpet blast

Into the Light

Instructions: The Gift

If you would speak, you must listen.
—Source unknown

i.
When the dog spoke, we could tell
he wanted us to listen
not speak until
given: the command.

We understood this was important
bore a meaning more significant
than even an empty dish
in the corner.

ii.
When the dog shouted,
he demanded our attention
insisted we stop what we were doing
that we listen.

iii.
When the dog laughed,
we joined him,
snickering as we rolled
in the sweet summer grass.

Optical metaphysics

Tom positions his tripod, aims his camera into leggy boughs
of the *daphne odora,* then calls out in surprise
at the power of its scent, an exhale released only at cooling dusk.

He wants us to come nearer, admire what he has found
captured in the eye of the lens. *The picture is so perfect,*
he starts to explain, *it's like something not real.*

Splayed there, a spider rides an ice-rimmed web
hanging in the careless breeze,
suspended as time feels tonight.

      Bound as we are by imperfect physics,
      not enough room to go anywhere fast.
      Not enough time to do anything right.

Full moon, April

tonight's moon so bright,
shining through the window

I can hear it – like a note
sung with your fingers

sliding round the edge
of a glass half-filled with water

its tone long and clear
cool and blue

The importance of the bird

i.
The bird is more than a song you never heard.

Its singing contains more
> than the forgotten sounds
> of all that winter knows
> the cold white stories
> that abide in frozen depths.

ii.
The bird is more than looping figure eights.

Its hungers rule its life, drive it to beat its wings
> through rain and wind and midday heat
> into blurry swarms of insects, swallowing
> without cessation.

iii.
The bird is more than heading into nowhere.

The map it carries in its head
> is broader than the world you have travelled
> on the two feet that carry you
> hither and yon and beyond.

iv.
The bird is more than dogs beneath the moon.

Its memory isn't crowded with furry recollections
        of days running thick as wolves in packs
        through sheaves of singing green grass.

v.
The bird is more than all that matters,
        bird knows sky.

Today is a day for yellow

Today is a day for yellow foods: scrambled eggs
and buttery toast, peaches by the side. At lunch, a bowl of soup:
made from squash and curry, flaked with coarsely grated cheese.

A day for lazy thoughts, maybe strolling
to the lake, taking in the last
of autumn's warm slanting lines.

For supper, cut-up chicken,
the comfort of stew, thick
and flecked with golden bits of carrots.

Later, a crossword I find curled amongst the kindling
parchmenty, as if out in the sun too long
infused with too much yellow light from such a blue blue sky.

Last fly, October

How must this white kitchen look
to those ten-thousand eyes?
How many sinks reflected, how many
cupboards, shining knives.
If I thought that you could tell me, I'd want
to capture you, trap your blue-black beauty
in some fantastic box, one with six panes of glass
for its sides. Maybe I could train you
to eat bits of salty meat, feed you
with a small tight pair of tweezers.
Hang on to you through winter, over
Christmas, Valentine's. Keep you as a gift
I could give away next spring.

Even the Starhip *Enterprise* is Being Grounded

We won't be remembered for traffic lights
or shopping malls, the number of gadgets
in our kitchens. I worry they'll remember us

for ruining the planet, for-
getting there'd be people here
after we're gone.

This morning's news announced our corner shop is closing
(a place where you could choose which clump
of raisins look the freshest, ask for only eighty grams,

please). And now my brand-new dictionary's headings
have assigned God to the same page as greed.
Next week they'll be scraping off the final episode

the last nest of ducklings from beside the quiet pond,
hidden in the park across the road. Making a space
where the Wal-Mart's going to be.

Caribou are falling
through holes in softened ice,
and look out. It isn't even summer.

My children still bring prizes for my birthday

They know that I have everything I could ever need,
so now they give me flowers, in bunches, tied with ribbons.
Others by the bucketful, scouted from backyards
between the springtime rains and wooden fences.
Daffodils and lilacs, a vase of rainbowed tulips, floppy as cottontail
   ears.

Some are even store-bought. Colourful *gerberas,*
leggy babies slooped in plastic straws. A blooming
African violet I will surely kill by June.

I have roomfuls of bouquets: mums with green salal,
leafing branches, buds and blossoms, mostly sunny tones.
Reminders of the noise and busy mess when they were small,
how then they brought me bunches of golden dandelions,
spilling out from tiny, sweated fists.

Guilt trip

Driving from the exit by the border down at White Rock
riding highway to the city, I'm alone.

A hitchhiker stands by the side of the road,
holds a cardboard sign I can't quite read.

I almost stop but don't – he is a man, too near
my age. He should have his own car, his own stink of fuel.

Instead I turn my thoughts to the roses that endure,
the ones I saw this morning, clinging by the shed, hanging

on despite this early snow. How cold they looked
against that white, pink as lonesome thumbs.

On the wane

the leaf remembers the moon
fading though it may be, receding into dark
as is the leaf itself,

perhaps more glorious now
dressed in autumn tones than in
anonymous hues of summery green

it basks in scarred light
cast by the cratered moon
each crevice reflected in ridges
of its own veined skin.

Mountains to Cross

Lakeside, summer afternoon

Humming insects gather, form a hovering cloud.
Ignoring their noise, I slouch in the saggy canvas chair, turn
another page

in the book I'm only glancing at, not really reading at all.
One of my feet dangles over the edge
of the dock like lazy bait.

Liquid skin of a silvery fish arcs
above the water. He holds for a second then glides back down
into the depths of cool.

And when the rain began to fall
against the face of the lake
how it erupted in pockmarks of drops,

hundreds of opening mouths, gasping like hungry fish
or tiny wet stalagmites,
pointing toward sky.

Cerulean pool, change room

The French call it bleu celeste, *heavenly blue.*
—Kassia St. Clair

I have learned to recognize
the shape of old incisions
can read the lines of scars:
appendix, open-heart
the zigzag left on thighs
where metal hips go in
the long frown where a kidney
used to hang.

I understand the petalled scrolls
of stretch marks on breasts
indigo scribbles of varicose veins
meandering past a knee

the puckered line on an abdomen
where a doctor once reached in
pulled out the baby coiled inside
that child now a mother herself.

These women in the change room
sit down to tie their shoes
use clothes pegs to pull up their socks
have devised ingenious ways

to lever on their underwear,
outsmarting the reach of their arms.
They take balance from the strength of walls
lean into them, like lovers, with grace.

I do my best to follow the steps,
mime their cautious techniques,
learn from them,
these subtle choreographies.

Prep talks

strangest days these truly are
my mother having visions
detailed conversations with her sisters

laughing with her brother Jack
speaking with her mother, tolerating
visits from even the in-laws

says she doesn't care if anybody's mad
doesn't worry what they think, then laughs –
knows they've all been dead these twenty years or more

tells me she's been having long discussions with my dad
my son remarks he hopes
they get along a little better

with shining eyes she tells us
she's ready to go, hears the rustle,
wings about to unfurl

Memento

Just before her death, the woman's body was transformed.
Its rigid flesh beneath the sheets turned supple,
almost lithe.

Hers were lovely dancing legs, thin
with pointed toes, frilled skirts riding
just above the knee.

In amongst the harmonies of polished violins, sawing
grand crescendos, comes the trill of flute
its lively notes could lure a bird
from its branch high in a tree.

Laughter of young girls playing at jacks, scraping
the sides of their hands on the walk, scooping
the leaden stars into the pocket of their palms, keeping them
safe to make ornaments, maybe haloes for Christmastime.

High-rise view, dawn

...a wisp of white cloud spiraling...
as if...a spirit were leaving a body
—Susan Musgrave

This morning, watching the city
start to fill itself with day
a gridded hillside of streetlights went dark, the closing of an eye
brought memories of my mother, explaining her view of Death:

a shutting-down of systems, as if they were Christmas lights
winking off by segments – first a string of blues,
then a row of sparkling greens, last those enduring reds.

But that wasn't how she left in the end,
hers was a gradual seeping. Invisible
rising of vapours, a sponge going dry, a slow giving-in
to the heat of the parched white world.

Wordsong

(remembering Miki, who left too soon)

Adib Adele
abed a bell

a star Estelle
alas too far

aslant afoot
a door ajar

akin alike
a three-wheeled bike

or nothing more
than Western Shrike

a thing so true
as morning light

a boat ashore
a bird in flight

this August day
a soul astray

Regenerative

today I planted tulip bulbs, measuring as I dug,
each an outspread hand apart,
a palm's breadth deep of open earth
beneath each oniony shape

so much implied in the planting of flowers
conviction that green tips will again suffice,
survive winter's icy claw, the diggings of frantic squirrels,
overcome the knotty roots of cedars gone astray

a belief that they will surface towards earliest warmth
that every holy bud will ripen as it rises, open
its blushing mouth, sing praises to the light, reassure my waning faith
in hope and second chances, reaffirm the promise of springtime.

All that I'm good at

Unsticking gooey cook pots, *lhude sing, hurrah.*
Picking rounded rocks that thought they were new potatoes
raking them from the garden with my fingers.
Talking nonsense to worms who rise with summer rain,
their scent a bitter metal, melted pennies in the hand.
I philosophize with robins who forage in the yard;
they tip their heads as if they may be listening.

These skinny wrists of mine were made for scraping guck
stuck between the corrugated racks inside the fridge:
a tray of too-warm Jell-O must have drizzled down the grooves
insinuating neon green into the white plastic wall
(a fluted shape, impractical, inspired by Martha Stewart,
a form that won't reflect a glare on YouTube cooking shows,
matte that schlurps up light, even better than the moon).

Rachel Carson heard the sound of now-impending silence:
Who would want to live in a world which is … not quite fatal?
Who would try to ride a screaming horse off a cliff?
I am good at hoisting jars onto pantry shelves, hoarding
for a day that may not come. Good at soups and stews,
making loaves from nothing but dust, mining flakes of rust
beneath the kitchen sink, emptying the dead mouse from its trap.

Today a long-lost pal befriended me on Facebook.
 I still have the sweater
she knitted me that winter, the year we all got pregnant
with somebody's baby. We went to all-day movies

just to be warm. These nights I curl beside you, we sleep
like burrowed bears. Even so, my dreams can still defeat me.
   Some nights I awake
to a galloping horse in my chest, taking me to an island in a lake.

Big Plans

In my next life I'll be a plumber,
someone who understands
the downward pull of gravity
liquid's spiral flow.

Someone who will mediate
the long complaining relationship
between water
and ageing copper pipes.

The one you can rely upon
to clear up complexities: a mass of hair,
some tangled thought, dead
in a neural maze – able to ease
the cause of poundings, loud
in papery walls, all
those taps drip-dripping
deep inside your skull.

The poem I am not going to write

The poem I am not going to write excuses herself
daily, needs to wash her hair, roust the dust-bunnies
from under the bed, empty the worn-out clothes
that malinger in her closet.

The poem I am not going to write promises
to pay off bills, clean up the pie juice
now baked into the oven, sort those mismatched socks
into almost-acceptable pairs.

The poem I am not going to write believes
the world wants happier messages, the children need prettier
sandwiches in their lunches, the books deserve better
poems than I can write today.

Notes on the Poems

"O dear angel": A guardian angel, a heavenly figure assigned to watch over particular humans, may seem out of place in the context of Dick and Jane. Names of the Catholic school equivalent children, David and Anne, seemed too obscure, so Dick and Jane it was.

"Doc Robin": reminiscent of illustrations in children's books by authors such as Thornton W. Burgess.

"Women understand the colour red": madder, sometimes called rose madder (as it was by novelist Stephen King) is a somewhat rare but ancient red dye. "...fabric stained with the plant's root was found in Tutankhamun's tomb." Cited by Kassia St Clair in her remarkable book, *The Secret Lives of Colour.*

"Poem of X, Y, and Z": EMDR (Eye Movement Desensitization and Reprocessing, usually pronounced 'em-der') is a non-invasive, chemical-free treatment for depression, especially Post Traumatic Stress Disorder. It involves the therapist leading the patient through a series of eye movements which often unlock suppressed memories.

"Gravity of the Situation": The Lee Building is a heritage structure with a history of court battles relating to the slowly-rotating billboard that stood on the rooftop for years. Despite many challenges, the billboard is no longer there.

"Green Tara intones the first notes of dawn in the forest": Green Tara, one of the female icons in Buddhist tradition, offers a counterpoint to the predominantly male images depicted in Buddhism. One of Sam Hamill's poems to Basho praises the body's nine holes, but anyone who is paying attention might notice that nine is the number of holes in a male body. Females are blessed with ten.

"Vanities of our Times": takes its inspiration from a trip to Costa Rica, though the situation is one that could, sadly, occur almost anywhere.

"Relentless": not as far-fetched as some may believe. My city, (Surrey, BC) is currently working on an official plan, seeking ways – including the possibility of relocating residents – to deal with climate change's inevitably rising oceans.

"River of salmon, river of dreams": The life cycle of the salmon consists of seven distinct phases, honoured in the first seven parts of the poem. The last three are meditations on the very real possibility that these iconic fish will go extinct. Part 4 makes reference to the Elwha River in Washington state. Dammed since early in the twentieth century, the old obstruction has since been deconstructed, allowing the salmon to return to their traditional spawning grounds. This action seems ironic, especially in light of the BC government's stated intent of building the dam at Site C on the Peace River, construction that will result in environmental devastation – for fish, birds, and mammals, as well as the loss of sacred sites and farmland.

"Wordsong": Miki was a wonderful Old World gentleman, a Hungarian who came on his own to Canada as a teenager and made a life here. On arriving in Montreal, he taught himself French, then came west, learned English, and earned a degree at UBC. He loved words and the possibilities for games they often presented.

"All that I'm good at": a roundabout, vaguely palindromic response to Jessica Hiemstra-van der Horst's "I ache sometimes, from loving this world so much, from loving" – a poem she circulated as a challenge/

prompt to writers, with those poems later included in a special
limited edition book, *Translating Horses: the Line, the Thread,
the Underside*. The Rachel Carson quote in this poem is from *Silent
Spring*.

Acknowledgements

There are always too many people to thank properly, especially with a book as long in the birthing as this one. Thus, thanks must go to those first early readers, Pam Galloway, Leona Gom, and Marion Quednau, and to the BC Arts Council whose grant helped me get to Banff where so many of these poems were conceived.

Over time, several writing groups have played a supportive role in my work: Three Little Piggies, the Chicks, Memoiristas, and P^6. These women know who they are, though I doubt they realize how much they have given me.

As for mentors and teachers – some likely don't even realize how much they helped: Dorothy Bock, Eileen Kernaghan, Elizabeth Philips, Anne Simpson, and Betsy Warland (VMI), to name a few.

I must also extend thanks to the artist Jian Jun An, whose remarkable painting fed my imagination over several years, and who allowed us to use that image for this book's cover.

I thank the broad community of writers – those who live nearby out here in the 'burbs, those in the city of Vancouver, and those across the country whose friendship and presence help sustain me.

Gratitude goes to Inanna Publications, especially Luciana Ricciutelli, Editor-in-Chief, and Renée Knapp, Publicist/Marketing Manager.

Special thanks must go to members of my family, who tolerate my oddball ways and various absences. And most of all to George, whose patient kindness and goodness serve to nurture me always.

Versions of the following poems have appeared in various publications, both print and online.

"Chasing the Light of Fireflies," *Canadian Poetries*.

"The Uncertainty of Machines," *CV2 Magazine*.

"Practical Anxiety," *Force Field: 77 Women Poets of British Columbia*, ed. Susan Musgrave (MotherTongue Publishing); Chinese versions in *Bei Fei Ming Magazine*.

"In Defense of Messiness," *Cascadia Review*.

"Spring Camp, Deep Creek," English and Chinese versions in *Bei Fei Ming Magazine*.

"Gravity of the Situation," *A Verse Map of Vancouver*, ed. George McWhirter (Anvil Press). Also in *Wordworks Magazine*.

"Heaven is some place and no place we know," *Green Stone Mountain Review*.

"In the name of the Lord," *Cascadia Review*.

"When God Came to Stay with Us," *Canadian Poetries*.

"Trilogy for Faith, Hope and Charity," *Inside/Out Magazine*.

"Beatitudes for the 21st century," *Igniting the Green Fuse: Four Canadian Women Poets* and in *Force Field: 77 Women Poets of British Columbia*, ed. Susan Musgrave (MotherTongue Publishing).

"Green Tara intones the first notes…," *Cascadia Review.*

"Portrait of a Forest" [part of a poem commissioned by the City of Surrey for the Mayors' Poetry City Challenge] posted in Blaauw Forest as part of the "Han Shan Project."

"Vanities of our Times," *Igniting the Green Fuse: Four Canadian Women Poets* (above & beyond productions).

"Night of the Bears," broadcast on CBC radio, Vancouver (NXNW program) and posted on League of Canadian Poets blogsite.

"Perseids/Nebulae," *Igniting the Green Fuse: Four Canadian Women Poets* (above & beyond productions).

"The Dreams We Take for Silence," *Igniting the Green Fuse: Four Canadian Women Poets* (above & beyond productions) and *The Revolving City,* eds. Wayde Compton and Renée Sarojini Saklikar (Anvil Press).

"Walking inventory," *Igniting the Green Fuse: Four Canadian Women Poets* (above & beyond productions).

"Even the Starship *Enterprise* is Getting Grounded": *This poem is sponsored by…* anthology from Corporate Watch, London, UK.

"Today is a day for yellow," 14 Sonnets [a calendar].

"My children still bring prizes for my birthday," *Fieldstone Review.*

"Cerulean pool, change room," *Quills Magazine.*

"Wordsong," *Alive at the Center,* ed. Daniela Elza (Ooligan).

"All that I'm good at," *Translating Horses,* eds. Jessica Hiemstra and Gillian Sze (Baseline Press).

"The poem I am not going to write," *Room Magazine* and *Force Field: 77 Women Poets of British Columbia*, ed. Susan Musgrave (MotherTongue Publishing).

Photo: George Omorean

Heidi Greco is a longtime resident of Surrey, British Columbia, where she has been involved as a literary activist. She writes in many genres. Her essays and reviews have appeared in magazines and newspapers. Her novella, *Shrinking Violets*, came out in 2011. Her poems have been included in many anthologies. *Practical Anxiety* is her third book of poetry. She occasionally leads workshops on a range of topics from ekphrastic writing to chapbook making. She enjoys puttering in the kitchen and in a range of crafts, and delights in foraging for edible tidbits.